John C. Maxwell

Learning to Become a Person of Influence

LEARN TO POSITIVELY IMPACT
THE LIVES OF OTHERS

LEADER GUIDE

Dear Friend,

What a remarkable privilege and exciting opportunity you have to impact people's lives! Remember that as you spend the next several weeks covering the material in this course.

You and I will be partners as we explore what it takes to become a person of influence. As you study and teach, you will reach new levels of knowledge and growth. I am confident that you will inspire others to reach those same levels.

The principles contained in this book have been tested and proven again and again. I encourage you to read, study and familiarize yourself with the ideas in this book on how to lead a group through this information. The suggestions provided are designed to make your job as facilitator as simple and effective as possible.

I have devoted my life to equipping people, and it is my hope that you will take as much joy as I have as you lead people to a greater understanding of who the best team players are, what they do, and, most importantly, how they can become like them.

Your friend,

[signature]

John C. Maxwell

The Leader's Role

As the facilitator, it is imperative that you are familiar with all of the material in this application series. We recommend that you thoroughly review each lesson and prepare well for each session.

You should emphasize that the participants should complete the exercises consistently to ensure that maximum benefits from the course are attained.

The most vital element for the success of this course lies within you. Your mastery of the content will make all the difference. This Leader Guide is designed to provide a framework for study and activity. It is up to you to:

- Ensure that the key concepts are understood
- Facilitate the individual group exercises
- Inspire meaningful discussion
- Initiate content application

    and, most importantly

- Establish an atmosphere for learning and change

Preparation will be somewhat unique for each facilitator, but we can recommend a proven strategy: spend time planning, preparing and practicing.

Overview

As the facilitator, you must be very familiar with this information — take the time to prepare. You have the flexibility to add group discussion questions, group exercises and apply other teaching techniques to tailor the course to your individual group.

Each of the lessons in this Leader Guide is designed to be presented in an orderly format. This is the order we suggest:

1. **Overview** — This is a brief summary of what you are about to view in the video. You may also use this time to discuss what participants learned from the previous week's reading.

2. **Watch the lesson** — As a group, watch the lesson that John Maxwell presents.

3. **Exercise** — At the end of each section, you are provided with an exercise that captures the essence of that section.

4. **Challenge** — This is the time to encourage them to go out into the world and put theory into practice. Remind them of the following week's reading and questions for further review.

Preparation

Step 1: Read the book, *Becoming a Person of Influence.**

Step 2: Watch the videos.

Step 3: Study all elements of this Leader Guide and the Student Workbook.

Step 4: Teach yourself the class. Work through each element just as your students will.

Step 5: Make sure that you have a workbook for each person in your group.*

Step 6: Study the mix of people who comprise your group. Try to anticipate their expectations and make notes on points you want to tailor or emphasize, develop additional discussion questions, and anything else you deem appropriate.

* Additional resources available at MaximumImpact.com.

Contents

SESSION 1

    Introduction 1

    Goals of this training 2

    Your influence inventory 2

    Influence Insights 9

SESSION 2

    I – Integrity With People 12

    N – Nurtures People 14

    F – Faith In People 16

    L – Listens To People 18

    U – Understands People 21

SESSION 3

    E – Enlarges People 23

    N – Navigates For People 24

    C – Connects With People 26

SESSION 4

    E – Empowers Others 28

    R – Reproduces Others 30

Learning to Become a Person of Influence

Dr. John C. Maxwell

SESSION 1

Introduction

Leadership is _____**influence**_____

Law of Influence —
The true measure of leadership is influence — Nothing more, nothing less.

Law of E. F. Hutton —
When the real leader speaks, people listen.

— *The 21 Irrefutable Laws of Leadership*

Increasing your influence = Increasing your _____**leadership**_____

There have been meetings of only a moment, which have left impressions for life, for eternity. No one can understand that mysterious thing we call influence... yet...everyone of us continually exerts influence, either to heal, to bless, to leave marks of beauty; or to wound, to hurt, to poison, to stain other lives.

— J.R. Miller, *The Building of Character*

Goals of this training

1. Help you better _____understand_____ influence.

2. Help you _____increase_____ your influence with others.

Your influence inventory

Q. #1: _____Who_____ do I influence?

Principle: As a leader, I attract who I am, not who I _____want_____.

List the top 3 characteristics of a person you want on your team.

1) _____

2) _____

3) _____

I would never belong to an organization that would have me as a member.

— Woody Allen

LEADERSHIP IS INFLUENCE...
NOTHING MORE, NOTHING LESS.
— JOHN C. MAXWELL

Do I influence... (Circle one in each couplet)

Leaders or Followers

Thinkers or Doers

Big Picture or Little Picture People

Self-Centered or Other Centered People

Positive or Negative People

Insecure or Secure People

Successful or Unsuccessful People

Casual or Passionate People

Givers or Takers

Eagles or Turkeys

Q. #2: _____**How**_____ do I influence others?

Principle: How I influence people will determine how _____**many**_____, how _____**long**_____, and how _____**effectively**_____ I influence them.

Methods of influence — from worst to best

1. _____**Force**_____ — There is no choice in the decision.

2. _____**Intimidation**_____ — "My way or the highway."

3. _____**Manipulation**_____ — There's a winner and a loser.

4. _____**Positional**_____ — We follow because we have to.

5. _____**Exchange**_____ — We both win something.

6. _____**Persuasion**_____ — We follow because we want to.

7. _____**Respect**_____ — We follow because of the request and respect for the influencer.

Q. #3: How _____many_____ do I influence?

Principle: As a leader, the _____number_____ of people who follow, is based on my level of influence.

Note: Everyone influences _____someone_____ .

Few people influence a _____lot_____ of people.

•—— Your Leadership Potential ——•

•—— Your Leadership Level ——•

The difference between these two lines is determined by our...

1) _____Leadership_____

2) Willingness to _____change_____

3) Desire to _____grow_____

Q. #4: _____**When**_____ do I influence others?

Principle: Our value and significance rises when we influence others at a time when it is needed _____**most**_____ .

~

There comes a special moment in everyone's life, a moment for which that person was born. That special opportunity, when he seizes it, will fulfill his mission — a mission for which he is uniquely qualified. In that moment, he finds greatness. It is his finest hour.

— WINSTON CHURCHILL

~

Napoleon understood this reality as well. He once said: "I have noticed in every campaign that I have fought — that there is a key segment of time, somewhere between 13 and 15 minutes in which that battle is won or lost. I focus on that segment of time, and I win."

Leaders are _____**readers**_____

They sense...

1) _____**Teachable**_____ Moments

2) _____**Breakthrough**_____ Places

3) _____**Catalyst**_____ Times

Breakthroughs occur in people and organizations when they...

_____**Hurt**_____ enough that they have to change.

_____**Learn**_____ enough that they want to change.

_____**Receive**_____ enough that they are able to change.

6   Dr. John C. Maxwell

Q. #5: _____Why_____ do I influence others?

Principle: _____Why_____ you do something will ultimately determine _____what_____ you do.

Right motives are crucial to people because leadership functions on the basis of _____trust_____.

Questioning your motive is different than questioning your character. Motives are usually attached to specific situations and are often short in duration. Character, however, is connected to the heart, and is with you in all situations. Therefore, you can have a temporarily flawed motive and still a solid character.

Continual wrong motives is a result of bad _____character_____.

Q. #6: _____Where_____ do I influence others?

Too often, people feel that they cannot influence others because they do not have a leadership position.

Remember, the position doesn't make the leader...

the leader makes the position!

Leadership mistakes often made by people in the middle of the pack

1. If I'm not on _____top_____, I can't lead.

   Leadership is _____influence_____, not _____position_____.

2. When I get to the top, _____then_____ I will learn to lead.

   You will be tomorrow what you are preparing for today.

3. If I were on the top, _____everyone_____ would follow.

   If people don't follow you now, they won't follow you then.

4. When I get to the top, I will be able to do _____anything_____.

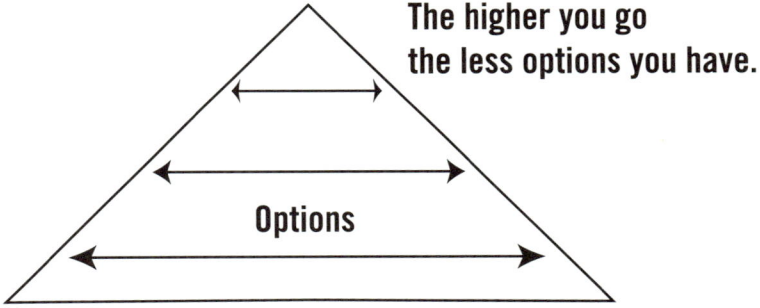

The higher you go the less options you have.

Options

INFLUENCE INSIGHTS
BECOMING A PERSON OF INFLUENCE

---

1. Leadership is __*influence*__ .

The very essence of all power to influence lies in getting the other person to participate.

— HARRY A. OVERSTREET

A Leader's Prayer

God, when I am wrong, make me willing to change.

When I am right, make me easy to live with.

So strengthen me that the power of my influence

Will far exceed the authority of my position.

— PAULINE H. PETERS

2. Our influence with others is usually not in __*all areas*__ .

Anytime you think you have influence,
try ordering around someone else's dog.

— THE COCKLE BUR

3. With influence comes _____responsibility_____.

There are people whose well-being and destiny are within a leader's influence. A leader cannot escape that fact.

Too many leaders want the _____perks_____ of leadership without paying the _____price_____ of leadership.

4. My influence with others is either _____positive_____ or _____negative_____.

~

My Influence

My life shall touch a dozen lives before this day is done,
Leave countless marks for good or ill ere sets the evening sun,
This is the wish I always wish, the prayer I always pray;
God, may my life help other lives it touches by the way.

~

5. Our influence can _____grow_____.

6. People of positive influence _____add value_____ to others.

~

A life isn't significant except for its influence on our lives.

— Jackie Robinson

We add value to people when...

1. We truly _____value_____ people.

2. We _____know_____ and _____relate_____ to what they value.

3. We make ourselves _____more valuable_____ .

4. We do the things that _____God_____ values.

Write the name of a person you want to influence _____

Leader's Guide Group Discussion Questions

As an assignment, ask the class to answer the following questions:
1. Who do you influence?
2. How do you influence others?
3. How many do you influence?
4. When do you influence others?
5. Why do you influence others?
6. Where do you influence others?

Understanding these important questions will help the class apply the lessons they will learn from this training course. Remind them to keep these answers in mind as they go through all the sessions.

Ask your class to list the areas in which they do have influence. Remind them that they will not have influence in all areas, but that they will need to focus on those areas in which they do possess influence.

INTEGRITY WITH PEOPLE
BECOMING A PERSON OF INFLUENCE

SESSION 2

An Influencer has...

1. I __*ntegrity*__ with people

In order to be a leader a man must have followers. And to have followers, a man must have their confidence. Hence the supreme quality for a leader is unquestionably integrity. Without it, no real success is possible, no matter whether it is on a sections gang, a football field, in an army, or in an office. If a man's associates find him guilty of phoniness, if they find that he lacks forthright integrity, he will fail. His teachings and actions must square with each other. The first great need, therefore, is integrity and high purpose.

— DWIGHT D. EISENHOWER

__*Trust*__ is the glue that holds people together.

In the business world it's acceptable to make mistakes, to lay eggs — big ones — but the Center for Creative Research, in a significant study, learned that one thing that sounds the death knell for those who aspire to the top rung on the ladder is betraying a trust. Virtually anything else can be overcome over a period of time, but once trust is betrayed, moving to the top of the ladder is out of the question.

Survey of 1,300 executives:

Q. What quality do you desire most in your team members?

A. ___71%___ said "Integrity"

Some years earlier in their Mission Statement they had a line saying that, "they would operate with honesty and integrity." Several weeks before the Tylenol incident the President of Johnson & Johnson sent a memo to all Presidents of Divisions of Johnson & Johnson asking if they were abiding by and if they believed in the Mission Statement. All Presidents came back in the affirmative.

The story goes that within an hour of the Tylenol crisis the president of Tylenol ordered all capsules off the shelf knowing it was a $100 million dollar decision.

When reporters asked how he could decide so easily and rapidly on such a major decision, his reply was, "I was practicing what we agreed on in our Mission Statement."

Integrity issues for influencers:

1. Does my organization have ___good written___ values?

2. Do the leaders ___practice___ and ___model___ them for others?

3. Do I place the interest of my people ___above___ my own?

4. Am I ___accountable___ to others for my actions?

5. Since I know myself best, do I like who I am?

*When I lay down the reins of this administration I want to have one friend left.
And that friend is inside myself.*

— ABRAHAM LINCOLN

Nurtures People
Becoming a Person of Influence

An Influencer...

2. N __urtures__ people

The height of your influence upon others depends on the depth of your concern for them.

Many leaders love their position more than their people. When that happens they soon lose their __position__.

Few leaders love their people more than their position. When that happens, leaders __strengthen their__ position.

Achievers care about people

Nice guys get the best results from subordinates, according to a study by the research outfit, Teleometrics International, as reported in the Wall Street Journal.

Of 16,000 executives studied, the 13 percent identified as high achievers tended to care about people as well as profits. Average achievers concentrated on production, while low were preoccupied with their own security.

High achievers viewed subordinates optimistically, while low achievers showed a basic distrust of subordinates' abilities. High achievers sought advice from their subordinates; low achievers didn't. High achievers were listeners; moderate achievers listened only to superiors; low achievers avoided communication and relied on policy manuals.

Notes on nurturing people:

1) Nurturing people does not mean __needing__ people.

2) Nurturing people does mean __commitment__ to people.

Love will find a way. Indifference will find an excuse.

3) Nurturing people does mean __*loving*__ people.

You will find as you look back upon your life that the moments when you have really lived, are the moments when you have done things in a spirit of love.

— HENRY DRUMMOND

4) Nurturing people does mean __*lifting*__ people to a higher level.

Jan Carlzon, chairman and CEO of Scandinavian Airlines, speaks from his experience when he suggests that there are two great motivators in life. One is fear. The other is love. You can lead an organization by fear, but if you do, you will ensure that people won't perform up to their real capabilities.

Deep down, your players must know you care about them. This is the most important thing. I could never get away with what I do if the players feel I didn't care for them. They know, in the long run, I'm in their corner.

— BO SCHEMBECHLER, *former head football coach, University of Michigan*

Faith in People
Becoming a Person of Influence

An Influencer has...

3. F*aith* in people

Assets make things possible

People make things happen

Every person is entitled to be valued by their best moments.

— Ralph Waldo Emerson

In leading others, there are three feelings that we cannot possess:

1) *Fear* — If we are afraid of people we cannot *confront* them.

2) *Dislike* — If we dislike people we should not *lead* them.

3) *Contempt* — If we look down on people, we will not *value* them.

Les Giblin, an authority on human relations, says that our actions must be genuine. "You can't make the other fellow feel important in your presence if you secretly feel that he is a nobody."

It is wonderful when the people believe in their __leader__.

It is more wonderful when the leader believes in the __people__.

Note: 1) Borrowed beliefs have no __power__.

2) We become __outside__ what we believe __inside__.

3) Lack of belief in people hurts both the __leader__ and the __people__.

4) The greatest gift a leader gives another person is to express belief in that person when that person doesn't believe in himself.

LISTENS TO PEOPLE
BECOMING A PERSON OF INFLUENCE

An Influencer...

4. L __istens__ to people

The first duty of love is to listen.

— PAUL TILLICH

A wise old owl sat in an oak,
The more he heard the less he spoke.
The less he spoke the more he heard,
Why can't we be like that wise old bird?

Climbing the "Ladder" to better listening

L stands for: __look__ at the speaker. Meanings are not in words, but in people.

A stands for: __ask__ questions. This is the quickest way to become a listener.

D stands for: __don't__ interrupt. It's just as rude to step on people's ideas as it is to step on their toes.

D stands for: __don't__ change the subject. Listening is wanting to hear.

E stands for: __emotion__ Check your __emotions__. Leaders must keep "current of the undercurrents." Emotions create a storm and others will back away.

R stands for: __responsive__ listening. When people feel that their leader no longer listens or responds, they will go somewhere else.

"4 H" questions to become a better listener

1) What is their _____**heart**_____ ?

2) What is their _____**hope**_____ ?

3) What is their _____**hurt**_____ ?

4) How can I _____**help**_____ ?

Are you a good listener? Take this quiz to find out

Good listening skills can make you a more productive worker. Take this quiz to see whether your skills need some honing.

Give yourself four points if the answer to the following questions is Always; three points for Usually; two for Rarely; and one for Never.

_____ 1. Do I allow the speaker to finish without interrupting?

_____ 2. Do I listen "between the lines"; that is, for subtext?

_____ 3. Do I actively try to retain important facts?

_____ 4. When writing a message, do I listen for and set down the key facts and phrases?

_____ 5. Do I repeat the details of an interview to the subject, in order to get everything right?

_____ 6. Do I avoid getting hostile and/or agitated when I disagree with the speaker?

_____ 7. Do I tune out distractions when listening?

_____ 8. Do I make an effort to seem interested in what the other person is saying?

Scoring:

    26 or higher: An excellent listener.

    22–25: Better than average score.

    18–21: Room for improvement here.

    17 or lower: Get out there and practice your listening right away.

Dr. Stephen Ash, "The Career Doctor"; cited in The Michigan Department of Social Services No-Name Newsletter, P. O. Box 30037, Lansing, MI 48909

None of us is as smart as all of us.

— KEN BLANCHARD, *Thinking for a Change* — April 2003

Understands People
Becoming a Person of Influence

An Influencer...

5. U**nderstands** people

Few things will pay you bigger dividends than the time and trouble you take to understand people. Almost nothing will add more to your stature as an executive and a person. Nothing will give you greater satisfaction or bring you more happiness.

— KIENZLE & DARE, *Climbing the Executive Ladder*

To understand the *mind* of a person look at what he has **achieved**.

To understand the *heart* of a person look at what he **dreams** of becoming.

Norm Wright says...

There are two basic reasons why relationships fail:

1) **Fear** which causes us to erect barriers.

2) **Selfishness** which causes us to focus on self instead of others.

Keys to understanding — leading people by reading people

1) _____ Background _____   5) _____ Relationships _____

2) _____ Personality _____   6) _____ Influencers _____

3) _____ Giftedness _____   7) _____ Context _____

4) _____ Keys _____   8) _____ Attitude _____

You have to see what others see — _____ relationship _____ .

Before they will see what you see — _____ leadership _____ .

Leader's Guide Group Discussion Questions

You have just completed the following segments in the course: integrity, nurturing, faith, listening, and understanding. Give the class an example of a successful leader who has influence. Have the class describe how that leader personifies each of those influencer traits.

As an assignment, have the class list action steps they can take to develop these traits.

ENLARGES PEOPLE
BECOMING A PERSON OF INFLUENCE

SESSION 3

An Influencer...

6. E __nlarges__ people

Q. How do you grow an organization?

Q. How do you grow people?

Success is...

__Knowing__ your purpose in life.

__Growing__ to your maximum potential.

__Sowing__ seeds that benefit others.

— *Your Road Map for Success*

There is no more noble occupation in the world than to assist another human being— to help someone succeed.

— ALAN LOY MCGINNIS

You'll always have everything in life that you want IF you help enough people get what they want.

— ZIG ZIGLAR

Navigates for People
Becoming a Person of Influence

An Influencer...

7. N <u>avigates</u> **for people**

The leadership surveys of Warren Bennis and Burt Nanus spell it out in black and white: "What we have found is that the higher the rank, the more interpersonal and human the undertaking. Our top executives spend roughly 90 percent of their time concerned with the messiness of people problems."

There are those who...

can see the problem ahead and <u>avoid</u> it,

can experience the problem and <u>fix</u> it, and

cannot see the problem or fix it and they are <u>overwhelmed</u>.

A leader is one who sees <u>more</u> than others see.

A leader is one who sees <u>farther</u> than others see.

A leader is one who sees <u>before</u> than others see.

Law of Navigation —

The Law of Navigation — "Anyone can steer a ship but it takes a leader to chart the course."

The 21 Irrefutable Laws of Leadership

Navigating for others means...

1) _____**Experience**_____ — Been there — done that!

2) _____**Success**_____ — Been there — done that successfully!

3) _____**Responsibility**_____ — I'm willing to take others on the trip.

4) _____**Communication**_____ — Encouraging — Honest — Continual

5) _____**Partnership**_____ — We go together — We help each other.

The man who goes alone can start the day.
But he who travels with another must wait until the other is ready.

— Henry David Thoreau

CONNECTS WITH PEOPLE
BECOMING A PERSON OF INFLUENCE

An Influencer ...

8. C __onnects__ with people

__Credibility__ + __Communication__ = Connection

Why people connect when they communicate

1. __Relationships__ — People listen because of who you know.

2. __Sacrifice__ — People listen because of what you have suffered.

3. __Insight__ — People listen because of what you know.

4. __Experience__ — People listen because of what you have achieved.

5. __Abilities__ — People listen because of what you are able to do.

6. __Intuition__ — People listen because of what you sense.

7. __Character__ — People listen because of your integrity.

8. __Humility__ — People listen because of your heart.

9. __Relevance__ — People listen because you identify with their needs.

10. __Convictions__ — People listen because of your passion.

Evaluation: Why do people listen to you? List your top two responses, from this list:

1. _____

2. _____

How to connect with people

1) Go to _____**their world**_____ .

　　Connecting with people means…Finding their agenda first.

2) Communicate from the _____**heart**_____ .

~

You've got to love like you'll never get hurt. You've got to dance like there's nobody watching. You've got to come from the heart if you want it to work.

— SUSANNA CLARKE, *writer*

~

3) Find the _____**key**_____ to their life.

　　Every person has a key to their life. When you find it, ask permission to turn it on…then turn it with integrity.

Leader's Guide Group Discussion Questions

You have just completed the following segments in the course: enlarging, navigating, and connecting. Again, use your example of the successful leader who has influence. Have the class describe how that leader personifies each of those influencer traits.

As an assignment, have the class list action steps they can take to develop these traits.

Empowers Others
Becoming a Person of Influence

SESSION 4

An Influencer...

9. E __*mpowers*__ others

Through these doors pass ordinary people on their way to accomplishing extraordinary things.

— Sign at WalMart Headquarters

Questions to ask before you empower others

1. Do I believe in people and feel that they are my organization's most appreciable asset?

2. Do I believe that empowering others can accomplish more than individual achievement?

3. Do I actively search for potential leaders to empower?

4. Would I be willing to raise others to a level higher than my own level of leadership?

5. Would I be willing to invest time developing people who have leadership potential?

6. Would I be willing to let others get credit for what I taught them?

7. Do I allow others freedom of personality and process, or do I have to be in control?

8. Would I be willing to publicly give my authority and influence to potential leaders?

9. Would I be willing to let others work me out of a job?

10. Would I be willing to hand the leadership baton to the people I empower and truly root for them?

Empowerment decisions I made concerning an assistant:

1) I determined not to know __everything__.

2) I determined not to know everything __first__.

3) I determined not to become the __primary__ source of communication.

4) I determined to let someone else __represent me__.

5) I determined to stay with my __strengths__.

Empowerment means:

1) __Seeing__ the potential of the individual and the proper fit for the job.

2) __Saying__ words that encourage, equip, and empower that person.

3) __Sharing__ your knowledge, experience and influence with them.

4) __Showing__ to others your belief in and power given to that person.

Reproduces Others
Becoming a Person of Influence

An Influencer...

10. R __eproduces__ others

No matter how much work you can do, no matter how engaging your personality may be, you will not advance far in business if you cannot work through others.

— John Craig

85% of the leaders attract __followers__

10% of the leaders attract __leaders__

5% of the leaders reproduce __leaders__

How can I reproduce other leaders?

1. __Model__ good leadership.

2. Provide leadership __training__.

3. Provide leadership __resources__.

4. Provide leadership __experiences__.

5. Create a __growth environment__.

A growth environment is a place where:

1) Others are __ahead__ of you.

2) You are still __challenged__.

3) Your focus is __forward__.

4) The atmosphere is __affirming__.

5) You are out of your __comfort__ zone.

6) You wake up __excited__.

7) __Failure__ is not feared.

8) Others are __growing__.

9) There is willingness to __change__.

10) __Growth__ is modeled and expected.

Leader's Guide Group Discussion Questions

You have just completed the following segments in the course: empowering and reproduction. Again, use your example of the successful leader who has influence. Have the class describe how that leader personifies each of those influencer traits.

As an assignment, have the class list action steps they can take to develop these traits.

Finally, have each member of the class give an overview of the lessons they learned during the course and based on their assignments, how they plan to continue their growth in these areas.

NEED MORE WORKBOOKS?
DO YOU NEED A LEADER'S GUIDE?

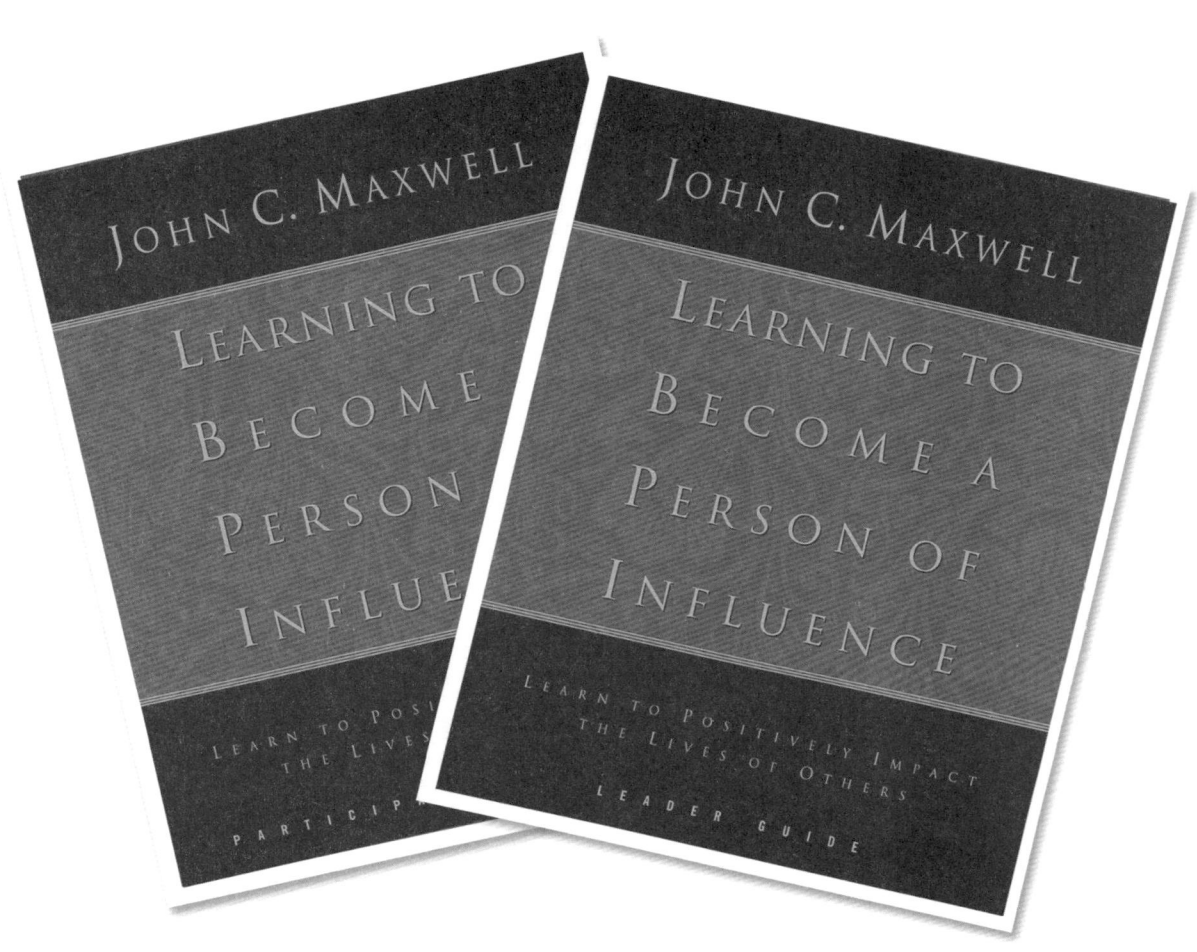

ORDER THESE RESOURCES ONLINE
AT MAXIMUMIMPACT.COM.

Notes

Notes